John F. Kennedy

by Vicky Franchino

Compass Point Early Biographies

Content Adviser: Professor Sherry L. Field,
Department of Social Science Education, College of Education,
The University of Georgia

Reading Adviser: Dr. Linda D. Labbo,
Department of Reading Education, College of Education,
The University of Georgia

COMPASS POINT BOOKS
Minneapolis, Minnesota

Compass Point Books
3722 West 50th Street, #115
Minneapolis, MN 55410

Visit Compass Point Books on the Internet at *www.compasspointbooks.com* or e-mail
your request to *custserv@compasspointbooks.com*

Photographs ©: Stock Montage, cover; Digital Stock, cover (background), 27; Popperfoto/Archive Photos,
4; John F. Kennedy Library, 6, 9, 19; Hulton Getty/Archive Photos, 7, 8, 10, 12, 15, 17, 18, 20, 21, 22, 23;
Morton Tadder/Archive Photos, 13; Victor Malafronte/Archive Photos, 14; APA/Archive Photos, 16;
Bettmann/Corbis, 24; CNP/Archive Photos, 25; DigitalVision, 26.

Editors: E. Russell Primm, Emily J. Dolbear, and Laura Driscoll
Photo Researcher: Svetlana Zhurkina
Photo Selector: Julie Barth
Designer: Bradfordesign, Inc.

Library of Congress Cataloging-in-Publication Data

Franchino, Vicky.
    John F. Kennedy / by Vicky Franchino.
       p. cm. — (Compass Point early biographies)
    Includes bibliographical references and index.
    ISBN 0-7565-0113-X (lib. bdg.)
    1. Kennedy, John F. (John Fitzgerald), 1917–1963—Juvenile literature. 2. Presidents—United States—
Biography—Juvenile literature. [1. Kennedy, John F. (John Fitzgerald), 1917-1963. 2. Presidents.] I. Title. II.
Series.
    E842.Z9 F73 2001
    973.922'092—dc21   2001001577

Table of Contents

A Young Leader

John F. Kennedy was the thirty-fifth president of the United States. He was the youngest president ever voted into office. He worked hard to make life better for people around the world.

Many people still remember November 22, 1963. That was the day John F. Kennedy was murdered.

◀ President John F. Kennedy

Early Life

John Fitzgerald Kennedy was born on May 29, 1917, into a big family. He had three brothers and five sisters!

The Kennedys lived near Boston, Massachusetts, in a town called Brookline. They were a rich family. Many people around Boston knew them very well.

John is kneeling on the left in this photo of the Kennedy family.

John's nickname was "Jack." He went to private schools in Connecticut. After high school, he went to **college** at Harvard University.

At Harvard

John liked sports. One day, John hurt his back in a football game. He had back pain for the rest of his life.

In 1939, John took a trip. He went to Europe. When he came back, he wanted to learn more about the world. He studied more and did well in school.

War Hero

After John finished college in 1940, he joined the U.S. Navy. World War II (1939–1945) had started in Europe. The United States went to war in 1941.

Serving in the U.S. Navy on PT-109

The navy sent John to the South Pacific Ocean. He was in charge of a boat called PT-109. In 1943, a Japanese ship crashed into the PT-109. John's boat

Getting a medal for bravery ➤

was cut in half. When it sank, John told his men to start swimming.

One man was too hurt to swim, so John pulled him through the water. He led the men to an island about 3 miles (5 kilometers) away. John was a hero. The U. S. Navy gave him a medal.

John's older brother, Joseph, was not so lucky. In 1944, he was killed in the war in Europe. It was a very sad time for the Kennedy family.

◄ John with his older brother, Joseph (right)

Working in Congress

In 1945, the war ended and John left the navy. For a short time, he worked as a newspaper reporter.

Then John decided he wanted to work in the U.S. **Congress**. But first he had to be voted into the job, or **elected**.

John ran for the U.S. **House of Representatives**. He wanted to represent

Signing up to run for Congress

the state of Massachusetts
in Congress.

Everyone in Boston
knew the Kennedys. In
fact, John's grandfather
had been the mayor of
the city. The family
worked hard and helped
John win the election.

John worked in the House
of Representatives for six

At work in the U.S. Senate

years. Then in 1952, he was
elected into another part of Congress called
the **Senate**. For eight years, he worked for
Massachusetts in the U.S. Senate.

More Kennedys

John Jr., who died in a plane crash in 1999, and sister Caroline Kennedy

John married in 1953. His wife's name was Jacqueline Bouvier. Over the years, they had three children—Caroline, John Jr., and Patrick. Sadly, Patrick was born too early. He died when he was only a few days old.

In 1954, John's back started to cause him pain again. He had a back operation to correct it.

While he was getting better, he wrote a book called *Profiles in Courage*. It was about brave Americans. It won an important prize.

John F. Kennedy and Jacqueline Bouvier on their wedding day ➤

JFK for President

More and more people heard about John F. Kennedy. Some of his supporters thought he should run for vice president in 1956. But his **political party** chose someone else to run.

Soon John decided he did not want to be the vice president. He wanted to be the president! The next election would be held in 1960.

John F. Kennedy's brother, Robert, helped him run for president.

Debating Richard Nixon on television

Over the next few years, John traveled a lot and gave many speeches. He talked about why he would be a good president.

On July 15, 1960, his hard work paid off. His party chose him to run for president.

John ran for president against Richard Nixon. The two men went on television to talk about their ideas.

Many Americans watched. Some thought John looked young and calm while Richard

John F. Kennedy gives a speech as his wife looks on.

Nixon looked pale and nervous. Television may have helped John win.

When the election was over, the votes were counted. It was very close, but John won.

A Family in the White House

On January 20, 1961, John F. Kennedy became the president of the United States. In his speech that day, he said, "Ask not what your country can do for you. Ask what you can do for your country." He believed that problems could be solved if people worked together.

The president with son John Jr. at the White House

John F. Kennedy was forty-three years old when he became president.

He was the youngest president ever elected in the United States. His children were also very young. There had not been little children in the White House for a long time.

The Kennedys made it a fun place for Caroline and John Jr. There was a preschool, a swimming pool, and a tree house.

John F. Kennedy with his family after being elected president

Problems Around the World

President Kennedy had many problems to work on. The United States was in a struggle with the Soviet Union.

The two countries were not at war but they often did not get along. They did not agree about many things.

President Kennedy with the leader of the Soviet Union, Nikita Khrushchev

The president with John Glenn, an American astronaut

The two countries were also in a race. It was a race to send the first man into outer space. In 1957, the Soviet Union won that race.

After that, President Kennedy wanted to be the first to send a man to the moon. He wanted to do it by the end of the 1960s.

President Kennedy also wanted to help poor people around the world. He started a group called the **Peace Corps**. The group sent skilled Americans to teach in poor countries.

Problems at Home

President Kennedy had work to do inside the United States too. In some states, laws treated black people differently from white people.

John F. Kennedy did not think these laws were fair. He wanted to pass a law that would give equal rights to everyone. The president worked hard on this problem.

These Americans called for equal rights for black people.

A Lost President

On November 22, 1963, John F. Kennedy and his wife were in Dallas, Texas. They were riding through the city in a car with an open top. All of a sudden, gunshots rang out. The president was shot in the head and neck.

The president was rushed to the hospital. He died a few hours later. Across the country, Americans were shocked and sad.

President and Mrs. Kennedy in Dallas on November 22, 1963

Vice President Lyndon Johnson became president after John F. Kennedy was shot.

The police looked for the shooter. They found a man named Lee Harvey Oswald. They believed he shot the president.

Two days later, Lee Harvey Oswald was also killed. A man named Jack Ruby shot him. Later, Jack Ruby said he did it because he felt sorry for the president's wife.

A Great American

President Kennedy wanted to make the world a better place. He did not have time to do everything he wanted to do. But some important things happened after he died.

In 1964, a new law was passed. It made sure that all Americans—black and white—had the same rights. In 1969, an American man became the first person to walk on the moon.

Neil Armstrong was the first person to set foot on the moon.

John F. Kennedy is buried in Arlington National Cemetery in Virginia. Every year, millions of people visit his grave. They remember the hopes he had for the future. They remember John F. Kennedy as a great leader. They remember a man who worked hard for his country.

John F. Kennedy's grave at Arlington National Cemetery

Important Dates in John F. Kennedy's Life

1917	Born on May 29 in Brookline, Massachusetts
1940	Graduates from Harvard University
1941	Joins U.S. Navy
1943	A Japanese ship sinks PT-109
1946	Is elected to the House of Representatives
1952	Is elected to the U.S. Senate
1953	Marries Jacqueline Bouvier
1956	Publishes his book, *Profiles in Courage*
1960	Becomes the youngest elected president of the United States
1961	Establishes the Peace Corps
1963	Is killed on November 22 in Dallas, Texas

Glossary

college—a place to continue learning after high school

Congress—a group of people elected to the U.S. government

elected—chosen for a job by a vote

House of Representatives—a group of Congress made up of people elected from each state

Peace Corps—a group that sends people to teach in poor countries

political party—a group of people with the same ideas about government

Senate—a group of Congress made up of two members from each state

Did You Know?

- John F. Kennedy's great-grandfather was a farmer from Ireland.

- In the White House, John F. Kennedy kept a coconut on his desk. He had used it to send a message for help when PT-109 sank.

- John F. Kennedy's daughter, Caroline, had a pony named Macaroni.

- For most of his adult life, John F. Kennedy had to wear a back brace.

Want to Know More?

At the Library

Adler, David A. *A Picture Book of John F. Kennedy.* New York: Holiday House, 1991.

Kent, Zachary. *John F. Kennedy: Thirty-fifth President of the United States.* Chicago: Childrens Press, 1987.

On the Web

The History Place: JFK Photo History

http://historyplace.com/kennedy/early.htm

For photos of John F. Kennedy from every stage of his life

Arlington National Cemetery: President John F. Kennedy

http://www.arlingtoncemetery.org/visitor_information/JFK.html

For information about John F. Kennedy's funeral and grave site

Through the Mail

John F. Kennedy Library and Museum

Columbia Point

Boston, MA 02125-3398

To get more information about John F. Kennedy

On the Road

John F. Kennedy National Historic Site

83 Beals Street

Brookline, MA 02446

617/566-1689

To see John F. Kennedy's birthplace and first home in Brookline, Massachusetts

Index

About the Author

Vicky Franchino received her bachelor's degree in marketing from the University of Wisconsin. She has written articles for newspapers and magazines as well as several nonfiction books for children. She enjoys the challenge of writing for a young audience. When she's not writing, Vicky enjoys reading, watching old movies with her three daughters, taking long walks with her husband, and eating chocolate ice cream!